FROGS

By Sindy McKay

TREASURE BAY

Parent's Introduction

Whether your child is a beginning reader, a reluctant reader, or an eager reader, this book offers a fun and easy way to encourage and help your child in reading.

Developed with reading education specialists, **We Both Read** books invite you and your child to take turns reading aloud. You read the left-hand pages of the book, and your child reads the right-hand pages—which have been written at one of six early reading levels. The result is a wonderful new reading experience and faster reading development!

You may find it helpful to read the entire book aloud yourself the first time, then invite your child to participate the second time. As you read, try to make the story come alive by reading with expression. This will help to model good fluency. It will also be helpful to stop at various points to discuss what you are reading. This will help increase your child's understanding of what is being read.

In some books, a few challenging words are introduced in the parent's text, distinguished with **bold** lettering. Pointing out and discussing these words can help to build your child's reading vocabulary. If your child is a beginning reader, it may be helpful to run a finger under the text as each of you reads. Please also notice that a "talking parent" 👄 icon precedes the parent's text, and a "talking child" 👄 icon precedes the child's text.

If your child struggles with a word, you can encourage "sounding it out," but keep in mind that not all words can be sounded out. Your child might pick up clues about a word from the picture, other words in the sentence, or any rhyming patterns. If your child struggles with a word for more than five seconds, it is usually best to simply say the word.

Most of all, remember to praise your child's efforts and keep the reading fun. At the end of the book, there is a glossary of words, as well as some questions you can discuss. Rereading this book multiple times may also be helpful for your child.

Try to keep the tips above in mind as you read together, but don't worry about doing everything right. Simply sharing the enjoyment of reading together will increase your child's reading skills and help to start your child off on a lifetime of reading enjoyment!

Frogs

We Both Read: Level K-1
Guided Reading: Level C

With special thanks to Erica Ely, M.S., Curatorial Assistant for Herpetology
at the California Academy of Sciences, for her review and advice
on the material in this book.

Use of photographs provided by iStock, Shutterstock, and Dreamstime.

We Both Read® is a registered trademark of Treasure Bay, Inc.

Published by Treasure Bay, Inc.
P.O. Box 119
Novato, CA 94948 USA

Printed in Malaysia

Library of Congress Catalog Card Number: 2019947744

ISBN: 978-1-60115-358-6

Visit us online at WeBothRead.com

PR-11-19

TABLE OF CONTENTS

Wallace's flying tree frog

Ribbit! Ribbit! Frogs are everywhere. They are amphibians (am-FIH-bee-inz), so their bodies are the same temperature as the air or water around them. They live on every continent except Antarctica. That continent is too cold!

Wallace's flying tree frog

Frogs can be green.
Frogs can be red.

Red poison dart frog

Frogs come in many different colors, patterns, and sizes. The smallest known frog is less than a half inch long. The largest is the goliath frog, which can be as **big** as a **small** dog! Another very **big** frog is the African bullfrog.

African bullfrog
(actual size)

The smallest known frog
(actual size)

Frogs can be **big**.
Frogs can be **small**.

The skin of a frog is very distinctive. It feels slimy and moist. Frogs breathe through their skin. When they **need** a drink, they take in **water** through their skin.

Frogs **need water.**

Wood frog

Frogs' eyes bulge out from the sides of their heads. This lets them **see** in almost every direction. They **hear** with ears that usually can't be seen.

Map tree frog

8

Ear

Frogs can **see** well.
Frogs can **hear** well.

Ear

Green tree frog

Most frogs have long, sticky tongues that are used to grab something to **eat**. They flick their tongue out and wrap it around a bug. The tongue then snaps back and throws the bug down the frog's throat.

 **Most** frogs **eat** bugs.

Green marsh frog

Frogs make a variety of noises—especially at night. Many frogs have a throat sac beneath their mouth that swells to make the sounds even louder!

Some frogs croak.

Green marsh frog

Painted reed frog

Some frogs click.
Some frogs grunt.

European tree frog

Green marsh frog

13

African clawed frog

Frogs have webbed feet for swimming **fast**. They have very powerful back legs for jumping. Some people have contests to see how **far** their frog can jump!

 Frogs can jump **far**.
Frogs can swim **fast**.

Wallace's flying tree frog

Almost all frogs can jump and swim. Their webbed feet help them to swim. Using long, strong back legs, many frogs can leap great distances. Many tree frogs use their webbed feet to help them soar and glide from tree to tree.

Dumpy frog diving

Wallace's flying tree frog

Some frogs can **almost** fly!

Adult frog with recently laid eggs

Tomato frog eggs

Almost all frogs start out life as an egg. Most eggs are laid in water. Soon the eggs hatch into **tadpoles**. Like fish, **tadpoles** have gills that let them breathe underwater. Some people think **tadpoles** look like giant **heads** with long **tails**!

Tadpoles

Tail

Tadpole

Head

Tadpoles have big **heads**.
Tadpoles have big **tails**.

Tadpoles

Masked tree froglet

As they grow, the tadpoles become **froglets**. The tail starts to disappear and legs start to grow. Soon they develop lungs. **Now** they can breathe air like we do.

Life Cycle of a Frog

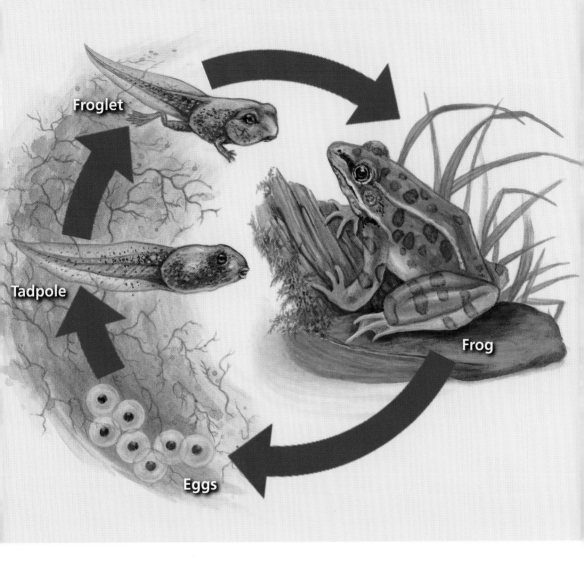

Froglet

Tadpole

Eggs

Frog

The **froglet** is **now** a frog.

American bullfrog

Toads and frogs are close relatives. In many ways they are alike. In some ways they are different. Frogs live near water and have moist, slimy skin. **Toads** spend more time on land and have **dry**, bumpy skin.

Common toad

Frogs must be wet.
Toads can be **dry**.

Cane toad

Red-eyed tree frog

Frogs and toads are an important part of the food chain. They are both prey and predator. Many have developed ways to avoid being eaten by **snakes**, lizards, birds, or other predators. One way is to climb high into the safety of a tree.

African bullfrog

Frogs eat bugs.
Snakes eat frogs.

Snake hunting frog

Woodhouse toad

Gray toad

Another way frogs and **toads** stay safe is through camouflage (KA-muh-flahj). The skin color and pattern of the animal allows it to blend in with the environment.

Vietnamese mossy frog

Can you see the **toads**?

Red strawberry poison dart frog

Harlequin poison dart frog

Green and black poiso dart frog

Some frogs and toads are poisonous. The poison is on their skin, so it can be dangerous to even touch them. They are usually brightly colored to warn their predators to **stay away**.

Three-striped poison dart frog

Blue poison dart frog

Red striped poison dar frog

Red strawberry poison dart frog

Dyeing dart frog

Stay away and do not eat me!

Yellow-banded poison dart frog

Golden dart frog, which may be the most toxic frog in the world

Some native people of the Amazon rainforest use the poison from these frogs to help them hunt. They make darts from palm leaves. The sharp end of a dart touches the skin of a frog to collect some poison. A blowgun is then used to fire the dart at the hunter's prey.

The frog is not hurt.

Wood frog

Water in a wood frog's body can turn into ice in the winter. When the ice melts in the spring, the frog is fine!

The dumpy tree frog is sometimes called the smiley tree frog. Can you see why?

A **glass** frog has skin on its **belly** that lets you see its internal organs!

Dumpy frog

32

Glass frog

The **belly** of this frog is like **glass**!

Panda bear tree frogs (Amazon milk frogs)

There are so many different kinds of frogs! The panda bear tree frogs have colors similar to panda bears. The Malaysian horned frog is camouflaged to look like a dead leaf.

The Argentine horned frog has a huge mouth that is almost half the size of its body.

Malaysian horned frog

Argentine horned frog

It eats lots of bugs!

Frogs are an important part of a healthy environment here on Earth. They help humans by eating bugs and helping to keep ponds and rivers clean.

Kids like frogs.

Frog on old tire in pond

Many types of frogs are in danger of dying out, and some are already gone forever. Their habitats are being destroyed to make room for roads, houses, and farms. Water pollution also destroys habitats.

Frog in polluted creek

This is bad for the frogs.

It is up to all of us to make sure that frogs have clean, safe habitats where they can continue to thrive. Healthy, **happy** frogs are a sign of a healthy, **happy** planet.

Red-eyed tree frog

Let's make the frogs **happy.**

Glossary

amphibian (am-FIH-bee-uhn)
an animal that spends part of its life cycle in water and part of it on land; frogs, toads, and salamanders are amphibians

camouflage (KA-muh-flahj)
a way of hiding by blending into the surrounding environment or background

habitat
the natural home or environment where a plant or an animal lives

life cycle
the series of changes in form and activity that a plant or an animal goes through during its life

pollution
harmful or poisonous substances in the air or water

predator
an animal that lives by killing and eating other animals

Questions to Ask after Reading

Add to the benefits of reading this book by discussing answers to these questions. If needed, you can refer back to pages in the book to help with the answers. Also consider discussing a few of your own questions.

1 What is the life cycle of a frog?

2 Can you remember any differences between frogs and toads?

3 Can you name any specific type of frog or toad? Can you think of anything different or special about it?

4 Why do you think it might be important for frogs to have good eyesight and hearing?

5 What are some of the ways frogs protect themselves from predators? Which way do you think is the best and why?

6 Why do you think pollution affects the health of frogs? Can you think of anything you could do to help frogs survive?

If you liked *Frogs,* here are some other We Both Read® books you are sure to enjoy! You can see all the We Both Read books that are available at WeBothRead.com.

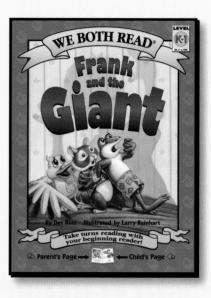

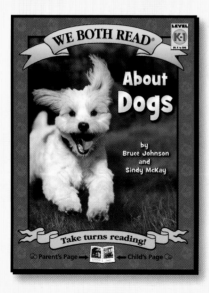

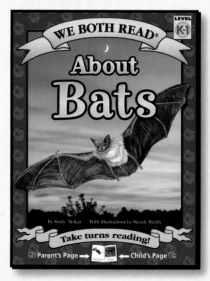